W9-BXT-267

GALLOWS SONGS

Gallows

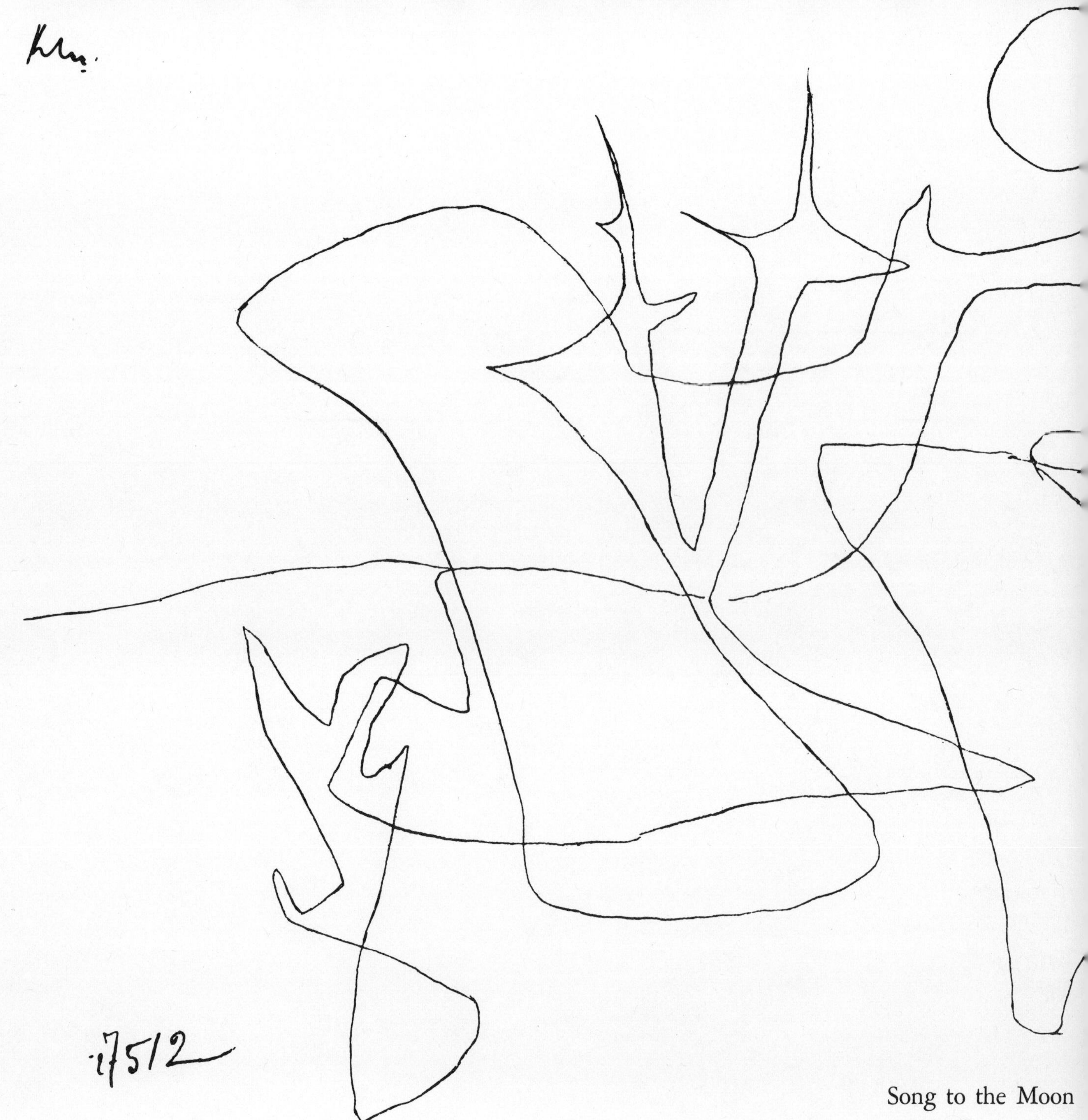

Song to the Moon

Songs

by

CHRISTIAN MORGENSTERN

Translated by W. D. Snodgrass and Lore Segal

Ann Arbor

THE UNIVERSITY OF MICHIGAN PRESS

Library of Congress Catalog Card No. 67-25337
Published in the United States of America by
The University of Michigan Press and simultaneously
in Rexdale, Canada, by Ambassador Books Limited
Manufactured in the United States of America

Both translators wish to thank the Corporation of Yaddo where we first met and began working on Morgenstern. We are also indebted to the Bollingen Foundation, which supported a number of these translations.

We are deeply grateful to those friends who have given constant criticism and encouragement; chief among these have been George P. Elliott and Rosemary Waldrop. Others have helped us with translation problems; one gave us a mistranslation so splendid we could not bear to correct it. We are grateful also to that person we cannot trace who wrote in the University of Rochester's copy of *Alle Galgenlieder,* the rhyme "the better a / et cetera."

Some of the poems first appeared in *New World Writing, The Quarterly Review of Literature, The Hudson Review, The Atlantic Monthly, Tri-Quarterly,* and *Modern European Poetry,* Bantam Books, N.Y., 1966. The following poems first appeared in *Poetry:* "Gull Song," "The Underpants," "Margaret, ii," "The Servant Girl's Dream," "The Midnightmouse," and "The Werwolf." The following poems were first printed in *Mademoiselle,* © 1961, by the Conde Nast Publications, Inc.: "Of Sculpture," "The Soundguard," "Korf's Clock," "Palmstrom's Clock," "The Theatre," "The Daynightlamp," and "Anxiety for the Future."

FOR PAUL STERN

Who taught the poems to Lore in German
when she was a child and helped us
translate them into English.

Contents

I

Palmstrom

Palmstrom, standing beside the brook,
Unfolds a handkerchief wide and red
On which a mighty oak is shown
And someone with an open book.

Blow his nose?—he would not dare!
For he belongs to that sort of men
Who are so often, nakedly,
Stricken by beauty, unaware.

What he has only just outspread,
Tenderly, now, he has to close;
No sensitive spirit will condemn
Him, marching on with unblown nose.

2

Blathersdorf

Palmstrom travels with one Herr von Korf
To the Double Dutch town, Blathersdorf.

Yet on this whole trip, cannot comprehend
One word, from the beginning to the end.

Von Korf, too (who kept Palmstrom company
Just for the rhyme's sake), finds himself at sea.

Precisely this, though, turns him pale with pleasure.
Our friend comes home enchanted beyond measure

And in his Weekly Chronicle writes this:
"One more experience crammed with bliss!"

3

The Questionnaire

Korf gets a printed questionnaire
From the police, sternly worded,
Demanding who he is and how and where?

Where was his last home? Precisely what
Day of what year was he born?
Divorced, married or single? If not, why not?

Has he received a permit to live,
At all, here? If so, why? Where does
His money come from? What does he believe?

Should the opposite appear,
He will be placed under arrest.
Beneath, two names are signed: Borowsky and Rear.

Short and sweetly, Korf replies:
"My dear most high commissioner,
The undesigning herein certifies

That after a personal inspection
He has the honor to present himself
Non-existent under the Legislation,

Prior, exterior and underhanded, with co-regret of
Proximitywise referentially discerned,
Korf. (To the police of the state of . . . .)"

This stuns the Bureau Chief concerned.

4

The Really Practical People

The really practical people come
Calling, today, upon Palmstrom;

They really stand, everyone knows,
In real life with all ten toes.

Slapping him on the back, they are
In almost every particular,

As they would say, completely his.
Yet he, who with his two legs *is*

Standing in real life, still must
Find out how much of this is just

—However well they mean by him—
An idealistic whim.

Worried, they shake their heads and cough;
Nearly twisting his buttons off,

They tell him of their fondest prayers:
He, too, will soon be one of theirs,

A personage of rarest sort,
A solid citizen, in short.

Group Interlaced

5

Korf's Sense of Smell

Korf's sense of smell is a mighty thing;
The neighborworld, however, lacks one!—
They say, "We don't smell anything";
And drive him nearly to distraction.

And so, like Stendahl, silently,
He writes this in his Diary:
Some day, when too much time has passed,
I shall be understood, at last.

6

The Olfactory Organ

Palmstrom constructs an olfactory organ
And plays on it Von Korf's "Sneezewort Sonata"

Which opens with alpine herbs in triplets,
Then charms you with an aria of acacias;

However, in the Scherzo, unexpected,
Between tuberoses and the eucalyptus,

Come the three notorious Sneezewort-phrases
From which this sonata has derived its name.

At each one of these "Ha-Cis" syncopations,
Palmstrom falls halfway out of his chair, while

Korf, at home, sits at his desk and safely
Hurls opus after opus onto the paper.

Note: Ha = B; Cis = F #.

7

The Aromat

Inspired by Von Korf's *Smell-Sonata,*
Friends have founded an "Aromata"

A refined place where, short and sweet,
You merely sniff, you'd never eat.

Coins are inserted; from the wall some
Horns emerge, fragrant as balsam,

And every balmy trumpet blows
Into the guest's inflated nose

The essence longed for; on a screen
Its faithful images are seen.

Myriads, in truth, partake a meal
For the first time with joy that's real.

Parable

Like a bough in the wind, Palmstrom sways. . . .
When Von Korf questions him why he sways,
He suggests that a lovely thought had lit
As a bird lights, delicate and swift,
Burdening him for a little bit—
And so, like a bough in the wind, he sways
Still swinging with the welcome gift.

Long Hair Soulful

9

The Mousetrap

I

Palmstrom hasn't a crumb in the house;
Nonetheless, he has a mouse.

Von Korf, upset by his distress,
Builds a room of trellises

And places Palmstrom therewithin,
Fiddling an exquisite violin.

It gets late; the stars shine bright;
Palmstrom makes music in the night

Till, midway through the serenade,
In strolls the mouse, to promenade.

Behind it, by some secret trick
A trapdoor closes, quiet, quick.

Palmstrom, before it, silently
Falls asleep, immediately.

II

Von Korf arrives in the early dawn
And loads this Useful Invention on

The nearest medium-sized, as it were,
Moving van for furniture,

Which is then hauled, by a powerful horse,
Nimbly, into the distant forest.

There, profoundly isolated,
This strange couple are liberated:

First the mouse comes strolling out,
Then Palmstrom—after the mouse.

The animal, with no trace of fright,
Takes to its new home with delight.

Palmstrom, meanwhile, observing this,
Drives home with Korf, transformed by bliss.

Korf's Clock

Korf builds a clock that has no peer;
It circles with two pairs of hands
Which point not only to advance
But also point back to the rear.

Does it say seven,—then also two.
Does it say nine,—then three, as well.
You need just one quick glance to tell
Time holds no terrors now for you

Since on this clock of Korfish-kind
Whose hands their Janus-pathway climb,
(Why else would it have been designed?)
Time is cancelled out by Time.

11

Palmstrom's Clock

Palmstrom's clock is of another kind,
To tender sympathies inclined—

Whatever you might ask will be approved;
Sometimes, already, she has moved

The way your heart profoundly pled—
Jumped either backwards or ahead

One hour, two hours, as much as three full hours,
Led by empathetic powers.

Clock she may be, with all her times; still
She would not ride a principle.

Let all be mechanism—for *her* part,
She is a machine—with heart.

12

The Soundguard

Palmstrom loves to wrap himself in noises;
Protection, partly, against outside sound;
In part, protection from a third ear.

And so he has had water pipes laid down
All around his rooms, which rush and gurgle.
Defended thus, he indulges often

In many long monologues, in many-hour-
long monologues, as that old orator
Of Athens roared into the loud sea-surges,
Demosthenes upon a strand of ocean.

Antique Figure

13

Putting the Clock Away

Exasperated by her tick, Palmstrom
Every evening puts his clock away
Under a glass with ether or opium.

He finds her all run down though, the next day;
So, to conjure her old spirits back,
Washes her out with mocha, strong and black.

14

To the North

Palmstrom's grown nervous; henceforth
He will sleep only to the North–

Sleeping to South, East or West
Provides the heart no proper rest

(If one's in Europe, you understand;
Not down South in some tropic land)

As a great scholar has asserted
By whom Charles Dickens was converted–

And, as we ought to take for granted,
From fixed magnetism of the planet.

Restoring his health, locally,
He trues his bedstead northerly.

In dreams sometimes, lined up this way,
Palmstrom can hear the Pole Fox bay.

15

Westeasterly

Korf, when he hears all this explained,
Feels himself to be mildly pained—

To him, it plainly stands to reason
That, because of the earth's rotation,

One must sleep with the center piece
Of the body strictly East.

Caustic, sarcastic, he will jest:
MY divan stays . . . . East by Eastwest!

Note: The final line contains an untranslatable pun on Goethe's "Der West—Östliche Divan," where divan means a conference of Eastern potentates or, by analogy, a book of poems.

16

The Demonstrated Healthsleep

Proving its famed health-giving powers,
Before 12 experts Palmstrom tests the theory
Of "sleep in the pre-midnight hours."

When, just at twelve, Palmstrom wakes up, he
Finds the experts all worn out and weary;
Palmstrom alone feels frisky as a puppy.

17

Of Sculpture

Palmstrom is sculpturing, it might be said,
Marble impressions from his featherbed:
Gods, humans, animals and demons.

Extempore, he grasps the eiderdown
Sacred to Plumos, springs back and examines,
By swinging lantern, his inspired caprice.

There in the interplay of lights and shadows
Palmstrom sees cavaliers, Zeuses, mulattos,
Madonnas, putti and a tigerhead.

He dreams: if sculptors actually created these
Works, they would redeem antique renown,
Outsplendoring imperial Rome and Greece!

Venus-Palmstrom-Anadyomene

Palmstrom wants, sometimes, to just melt away
As salt dissolves into a glass of water—
After the sun goes down, especially.

Till sunrise, he would like to rest that way,
And then again to step out of the water—
Venus-Palmstrom-Anadyomene. . . .

Confused Siesta

19

The Spheres

Palmstrom takes some paper from a drawer,
Distributing it artfully around the floor,

And after he has formed it into tight
Spheres, artfully distributed for the night,

He so distributes (for the night) these spheres
That he, when he wakes up suddenly in the night,

That he, waking in the dead of night, then hears
Paper crackling and a secret shuddering fright

Attacks him (so that in the night terrible fears
Attack him) being spooked by packing-paper spheres.

Palmstrom to a Nightingale
Which Would Not Let Him Sleep

Why do you not transform
Yourself to a fish; and,
In this matter of song, perform
Accordingly? For otherwise,
Through the long nights, how can
Slumber restore my eyes,
And blossom on my pillow,
Which is most needful? Then,
Do; if you are a noble fellow.

And your wife, too, on the nest—
How sweetly you will astound her
When you shine forth like a flounder
Blissfully at rest
On the top branch of your tree—
Or when you flutter around her
Like a flying mackerel,
Heavenly Philomel,—
You will do me this courtesy?

21

Delayed Action

Korf invents some jokes of a new sort
That only many hours later work.
Everybody listens to them, bored.

Yet, like some still fuse glowing in the dark,
You wake up suddenly that night in bed
Beaming like a baby newly fed.

22

The Indoor Air

Korf invents an indoor air
Which is so corpulent that ever
-ything in it will stay stuck there.

Right in the middle, like the feather-
holder with which he wrote no more
after that loud blow on his door.

He gives it an alibi; whether
In mid-air or else somewhere
In it, no matter how or where.

23

The Daynightlamp

Korf has a daynightlamp,
His own invention, which
At one flick of the switch,
Turns day, however bright,
To blackest night.

When, at the convention
He displays it on the ramp,
No man of comprehension
Who understands his field
Can fail to see, revealed–

(Brilliant day turns to night;
Applause storms through the house;)
(Someone starts to shout
For the janitor, Mr. Camp:
"Lights!" "Lights!")–to see, outright,

The facts: aforesaid lamp,
Indeed has powers which
At one flick of the switch
Turn any day, how bright,
To blackest night.

24

The Spectacles

Much and rapidly is the way
Korf likes to read. He loathes the play
Of matter needlessly over-ampled,
Out-rollered twelve times, and flat-trampled.

For settling most things, six to eight
Words are more than adequate;
While in as many sentences, you
Can chatter tapeworm-wisdom, too.

And so, Korf's genius invents
Something that comes to his defense—
Spectacles whose power collects
And pulls together verbose texts.

E.g., this verse you look upon—
So spectacled, it would be—gone!
Three and thirty suchlike are c-
ompressed into—one—questionmark!

25

Europe's Books

Korf goes to pieces when he sees
Europe's books; he looks, then flees.

He just can't think how anyone
Can suffer volumes by the ton.

Spirit thus—which makes him shudder—
Is banished to a grave of matter.

Spirit is light, its habits sprightly;
It should go, therefore, clad lightly.

But Europeans find no rest
Till, in boards, they've bound it fast.

26

Korf Bound

Korf gives instructions that they are to bind
Him in a book–to keep it by his side.
The two backs come together there behind
But in the front the book is opened wide
So that he, wing-burdened as it were,
Wanders along with pages fluttering
Behind his sleeves, or sometimes he'll prefer
To lie at rest while thumbing through his wings.

27

On Newspaper Reading

Korf often meets acquaintances filled with rage or sorrow
By the so-called world situation. Here's his advice:
Just read the papers for the day after tomorrow.

Suppose in Spring, the diplomats should start a brawl
You merely take up into hand a leaf from Fall,—
You'll read in that how everything came out, after all.

No doubt, we usually make the opposite application
And what would become of "Our Times" in *that* situation.
Yet, *de facto* these are all mere matters of fashion.

28

Pictures

Pictures can change values wondrously
Hanging upside down; that is to say,
With the head down and the feet up; this way
They're raised into the realm of phantasy.

Palmstrom, who knew this even in his youth,
Accordingly has the walls of a room filled,
And, as a painter of great objects, thrilled,
Discovers there, new truth after new truth.

29

L'Art pour l'Art

The fluttering of a sparrow startled into flight
Inspires Korf to a work of art
Created from expressions, gestures, glances—
Nothing else. They come with apparatus
To record it; but Von Korf "recalls
The work no longer"; does not remember any work
On the occasion of "an agitated sparrow."

Theatre

Palmstrom thinks this up: a brand
New theatre, with four sides and

(Hearing this, Korf is stricken dumb!)
A revolving auditorium.

Four times the poet's world is changed;
Four times you are rearranged;

Upon four stages, deep and wide,
Realest reality is spied.

For in this quadrature where
Only one drama every year,

It goes without saying, every act
Is realistically attacked.

Walls built from real stones appear,
Brooks that murmur, cool and clear,

You smell the soil that clogs men's boots,
Grass and trees bloom from actual roots.

Everything stands for one whole year
And so is truly real here.

He makes a model of the thing:
Out of tinfoil shapes a spring,

From matchboxes, a village neat,
And offers this to Kori—complete.

Korf and Palmstrom Compete in Nocturnes

1. The Priestess

Pensively nods, in twilight, the pagoda. . . .
Nearby, from the gateway of her Order
Tang-ku-ei-i steps out, ordained to guard her
Lands from onerous Life, from Death so odious.
Out of her mouth, there hangs the Moonlight Ode
Of Emperor Tang Wang, with its flowery border;
For with both hands she carries, from her larder,
One biscuit topped by a tiny oak commode.

She wanders over seven tremblingly narrow
Temple bridges, curved of flute-wood trestles,
To the moon-murdered hound's funereal barrow;
There, she breaks cake crumbs in the sacred vessels,
Tempting the moon to stoop down toward these coffers
And to the verses she, with her pursed lips, offers.

[V.K.]

Korf and Palmstrom Compete in Nocturnes

II. The Blouse

Though worn by day, the blouse
Rests silently at eve,
While through its hollow sleeve
There trots the mouse.

Through its hollow sleeve
Trots ghostlily the mouse
While, worn by day, the blouse
Takes rest at eve.

It rests, the dayworn blouse,
Still, in the lap of eve,
It rests, while through its sleeve
There trots its mouse.

[P.]

33

Korf and Palmstrom Compete in Nocturnes

III. Nocturne in White

The family, stony, chilly
And carved of marble white,
They kneel around a lily,
A ring around a lily,
In deathlysilent night.

The lily's white is frailer
Than is the marble's white;
The lily's white is frailer,
But marble's white is paler
In glimmering moonlight.

The family, the lily,
The moon's soft splendorlight,
They keep their vigil stilly,
Compete in watching chilly
In the deathsilent night.

[V.K.]

34

Korf's Enchantment

Korf has a distant aunt, you know,
An aunt who's an enchantress;
He hears it rumored she can blow
Out of herbfroth, planets.
He hurries to Odeliseloe
Straight to the enchantress.

He finds her wandering, asks her who,
Asks if she be the she
Who out of herbfroth planets blew,
If she's the faëry
The fairy from Odeliseloo
True, she *is* that faëry.

Both bowl and straw she's glad to place
In Korf's two hands, who puffs
Till, see there, right before his face
A loveliest sphere swells up,
Swells like a cosmic globe in Space,
Not some mere dream and fluff.

The sphere breaks off the straw, and calm
And gently floating higher,
Revolving, joins the cosmic psalm,
The planets' heavenly choir—
Those sounds that like a shepherd's shalm,
Urgent and soft, expire.

Within its global looking-glass
Von Korf soon comes to find
What each glad hour has brought to pass
Or moved within his mind;
Von Korf sees, there, his world—aghast,
Enchanted and spell-blind.

He calls his aunt his only Muse
And see here, and see there!
Something has rapt him from his shoes
And grasped him by the hair,
Kidnapped from Odeliseluse
To a New World in air. . . .

35

Speculative

Palmstrom finds he's fond of seeing things
In mirrors; most especially, those damp
Light vapors in the crystal ground are pleasing.

Before it, Palmstrom can divine the wings
Of Maja's nature. For this scamp of scamps,
The world dissolves into—a mouth—breathing—

Anxiety for the Future

Korf, whom inklings easily attack,
Can already see the skies
Filled with balloons of every size,
So all day he prepares whole stacks
Of draughts—the bylaws and statutes
Of a society for resolute
Maintenance of a zone designed
To keep balloon-caprice confined.

Yet as he writes he can smell doom:
His club already fallen behind;
The air, it seems to him, turns blind
And all the landscape gloom and tomb.
Therefore he puts down his pen,
Turns on his light (they *all* will, THEN!)
And hurries off to Palmstrom's place;
They sit together, face to face.

After four long hours, finally,
This nightmare is overcome.
First to break the spell is Palmstrom:
"Be a man now, Korf"; says he,
"You've laid hold of the wrong era;
What is this but some vain chimera
That tricks your intellect away
Bobbing over your head today."

Korf recovers his own clear sight–
No one is flying in the golden light!
He snuffs his candle, silently;
Then, points to the sun suddenly,
Saying: "If not today, sometime!
One day you will no longer shine,
At least for us–it makes one's teeth
Chatter–the masses underneath! . . . ."

Thereafter, Von Korf once again
Sits in his room and takes his pen
Drawing up a vast design
For the protection of sunshine.

37

In Good Faith

Palmstrom strolls through a strange town
"Dear Lord!" he thinks, "it's pouring down!"
And opens his umbrella out.
Yet, in the Heavens nothing occurs;
No leaf, inspired by breezes, stirs.
Still, one might harbor such a doubt
Since artful magistrates applied
Sprinklers to the walk beneath his stride.
The traffickings of this guest are bonafied.

38

Palmstrom Gives Praise

Palmstrom greatly praises nasty weather—
Then, things are much more quiet on the earth:
Commotions willingly pull themselves together;
Man walks with dignity, and knows his worth.

Even the umbrella's little sky
Symbolically acts upon man's core
Because the real heavens are still high,
Far from this swarming—Ah, and so much more.

In meadows, through the streets, across the common,
Palmstrom wanders while the torrents fall,
Delighted by this image of the human
That can behave so cosmo-logical.

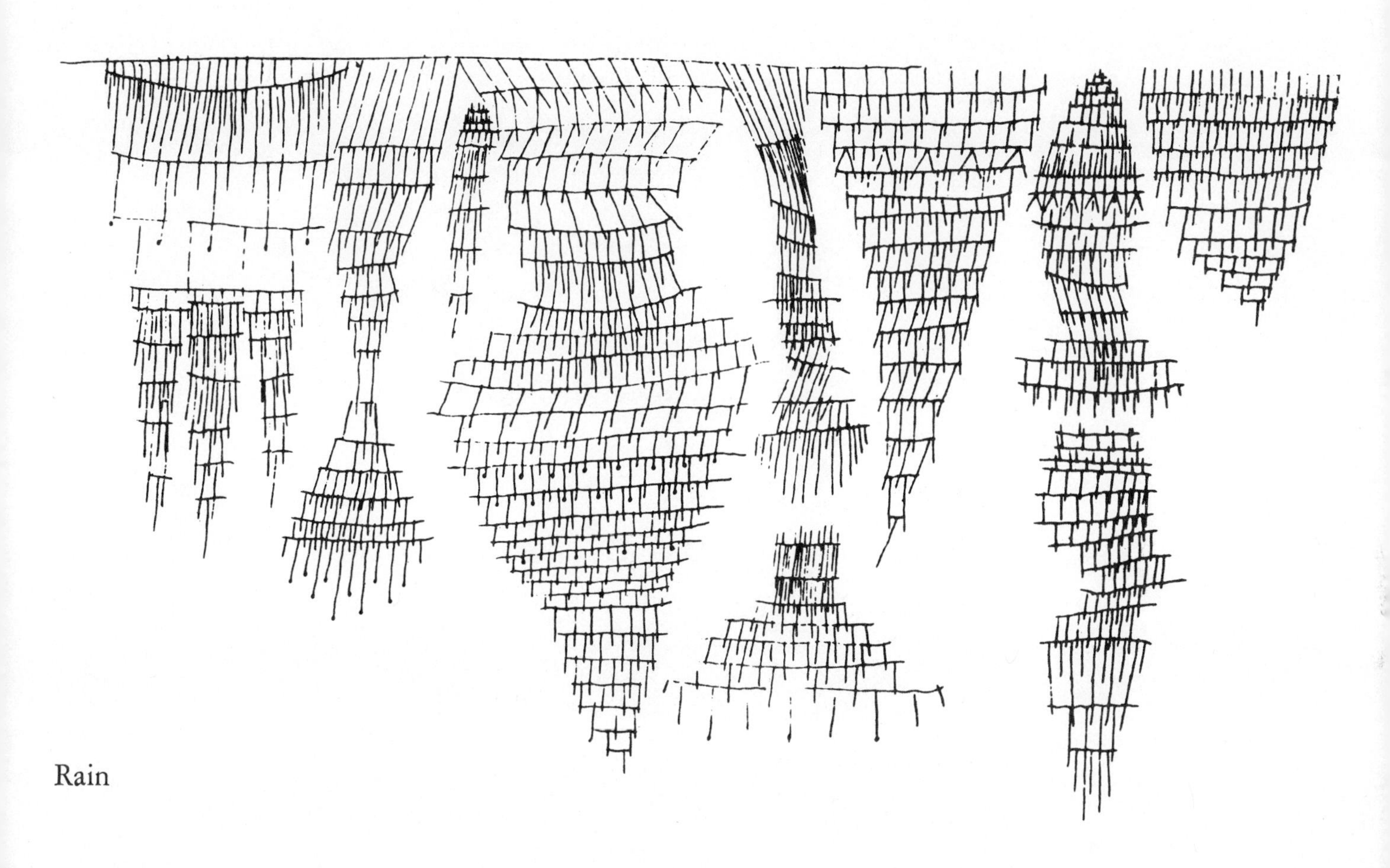

Rain

39

The Dreamer

Palmstrom stands candles up in bunches
On his bedtable's marble top
And keeps track of their dissolution.

Strangely they form mountain ranges
From the lava trickling down,
Creating tongues, and slugs, and topknots.

Winking high above the current
Stand the tall wicks with their torches
Swaying like cypresses of gold.

There do this dreamer's eyes behold
On the fabled white escarpments
Undaunted myriads of the sun's pilgrims.

40

Alpinism

I

Palmstrom computes with Korf, at home,
The cubic content of the Alps—for he
Conceives the Alps to be
A cube of tourists, cows and stones.
He fixes its approximate height
At 63 kilometres; and climbs
(Not traveling as at other times)
But spiritually, many a July night;
190,000 feet he lies
Over Tschirn, seeing the stars, fistsize.

41

Alpinism

II

(*Applied Science*)
Palmstrom conceives the Alps to be a cube
And climbs it through his telescopic tube.

Sixty-three hundred hectometres in air
Above apartment-level, standing there,

He sees the gaseous fleet of the corona
And there perceives the Moonsheep, *in persona.*

42

The World Resort

Palmstrom founds a world resort:
At the still point of a mountain's crown
He promulgates a windproof zone
For cures as well as sport.

That is to say that the hotel
Is built in a huge centrifuge, whose force
Hurls every wind back to its source
And can all storms repel.

There no wicked Northwind enters;
No evil Southwind wreaks its powers;
How fair the unturning center flowers—
The place to go—especially in winter.

43

In the Winter Resort

To end the sparrows' shivering,
Palmstrom has created
A factory delivering
The previously stated

Sparrows antistorm
Armoring in the form
Of ulsters, fur coats, hoods,
Warm mufflers, and such goods.

Now down the esplanade
And by the bandstand, see
How smugly they promenade
Strutting stiltedly.

44

In Beastwear

Palmstrom is fond of animal imitations
And trains two youthful tailors
Exclusively for beast costumes.

Thus, e.g., he likes to perch as raven
In the topmost branches of an oak
Keeping watch upon the heavens.

Often, also, as a St. Bernard,
He lays his shaggy head on his brave paws,
Barks in his sleep and dreams: Saved Wanderers.

Or spins a net inside his garden
Out of string and, as a spider, sits
Daylong in its middle.

Or swims, a goggle-eyeing carp
Round about the fountain of his pond
Letting the children feed him.

Or dangles himself, got up as a stork
Under the gondola of a blimp,
And makes off so, for Egypt.

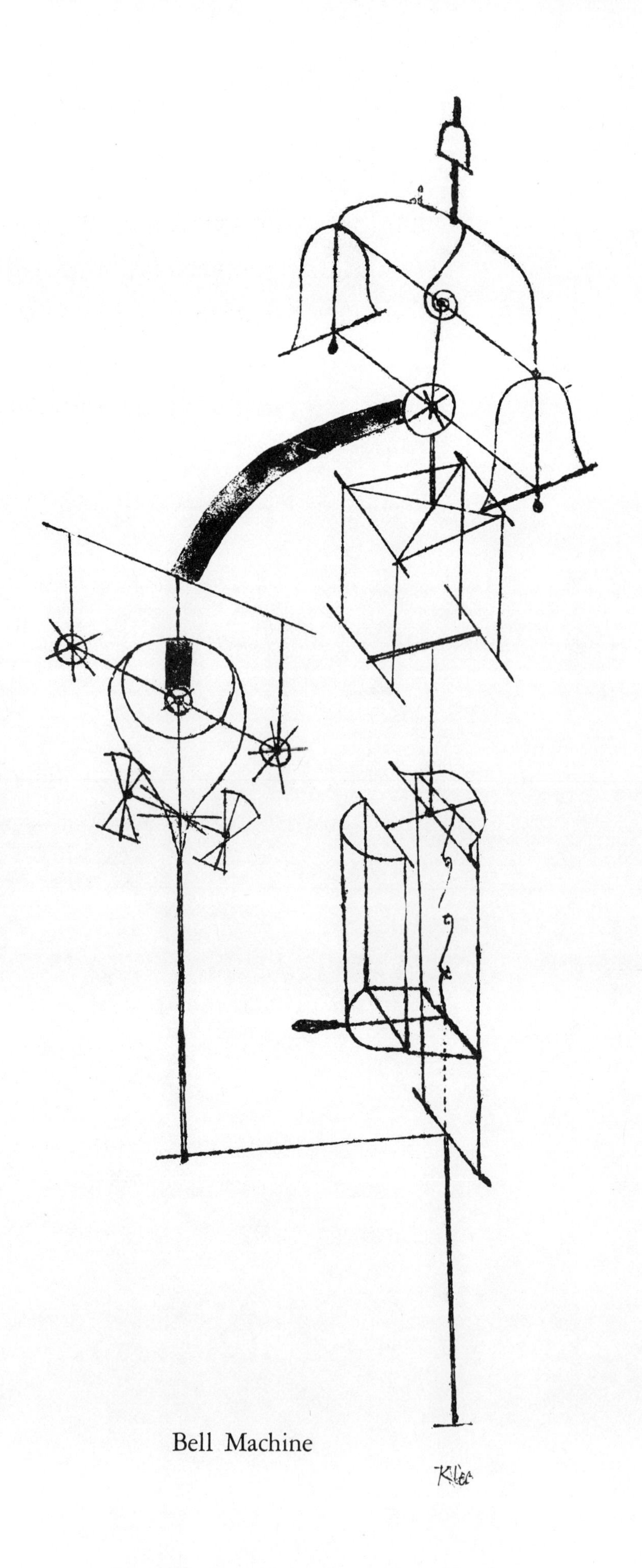

Bell Machine

45

The Scales

Korf, by good luck, happens to have found
Some way to build a musical human-scales
With glockenspiel announcement, pound by pound.

A body is determined by his song;
Even the tiniest personage just born
Can hark to his own weight in silvergong.

Von Korf, alone, gives off no melody
Since, you know, nonexistent in the sense
Of weighty and substantial citizenry.

The Not-To-Be-Resisted Tree

Palmstrom has a capsule built,
Buys alum, has the capsule filled,

And plants it in his garden plot
Then sits back for his seed to sprout.

The sun shines warm; the rain falls wet;
Earth takes it in her stride, will let

Herself be fooled, or thinks, "Well, *he*
's amused; it's all in a day's work to me."

She, from that capsule's neck, lets vault
An alumshoot, slim, full of salt,

Which growing quite incredibly
Becomes a tall and splendid tree.

Success can't summer-salt *him,* he
Lets it be gargled, A to Z,

By all with flu, colds or catarrh.
The town votes him: Most Popular.

47

The Emporium

Without mail, Palmstrom would pass away;
It is his meat and drink each day.

Three times a day, he feels all tense;
Every day, that same old dance.

How seldom does a letter slide
Into his mailbox, deep and wide.

He darkly squints at the mailman
Who, we know, does what he can.

Desperate, finally, he writes
"The Emporium for Small Delights."

Fresh from the grill, he makes his order:
Mixed Mail—enough to last a quarter.

Now, dawn to sunset, without fail,
Comes every kind and class of mail.

People all think of him and write
To keep him in touch, noon and night.

He sees himself suddenly enter
The world of things at their dead center;

Already he feels addled, sore—
The "E. for S.D."—nothing more.

The Castaway Musket

Palmstrom, wandering one evening,
Singing, roaming through the rye,
In the tall grain
Finds a musket.

Sadly, he breaks off his chanting
And, in poppies, sits him down
There to ponder
On his find.

He feels deep for that despairing
One who threw it in the rye,
Mourning for him
From the heart.

His hand, meantime, quietly winds
Poppies, grain, and blue cornflowers
Round the barrel,
Stock and trigger . . .

Then he leans the flintlock, thus
Wreathed, against the crossroads-stone
With a tender
Hope the faint-heart

Passing that way once again
Might perceive it there—and—
(. . . See the moon, huge
In the East . . .)

Note: Throw the musket in the rye— equivalent to throw in the sponge or throw in the towel.

49

Korf in Berlin

In his travels, Korf, accommodated
On the train of current affairs, comes to Berlin.
There, all of the best people ask him in
Though no one ever sees him, incarnated,

Since, in the flesh, as demonstrated,
He neither is mascul- nor feminine,
But virtual Spirit, as he's always been.
Thus, nevèr to be seen's pre-destinated.

50

The Pious Giant

Korf gets to know a giant
Whose wife puts anything she does not like inside
His mouth. Night or day,
Whenever she announces such
Intentions, one will see him, patient and compliant,
Open wide
The hedge of his teeth, then carefully
Push in everything that's in the way
Of his wife. And there is much
In the way of that woman. It would be quite impossible to say
Exactly what, from mammoth to mosquito, she
To some degree
Dislikes. Within that place
One sees whole streets, completely populated towns,
Mountains, rivers, gardens; not to mention gowns,
Plates, wigs, canes, beards. Short and sweet,
A complete
World collects in the aforesaid space.
Von Korf displeases; is taken quietly into the mouth
Of that pious, giant spouse.
Only because, as noted previously, he
Is a spirit, has Von Korf gone free.

Not Pleased

51

Palmstrom Becomes a Citizen

I

Palmstrom refuses (as we might expect)
Any form of military service.
This act's abused by most as cowardly and abject.

For everyone around is Catholic, still,
Or Protestant, etc.; and
A man is still thought diabolical who will

Not murder any Christian fellow when
God, the king, and fatherland command.
Palmstrom is arrested, there and then.

II

In jail sits Palmstrom, true and brave,
But tells himself this: Into jail
Should every man who is no slave.

Every truly unfettered soul
Should make sure not to miss this spot—
For *him*, the only worthwhile goal.

The liberated shall not wince,
Shall not complain, but duck his neck
Under the yoke of power, since

Man's mainstream, thus, also may be
—At first astounded, then through thought—
Clarified toward liberty.

III

Korf passes through the midst of guards
Who eagerly grasp after him.
All they can grasp is empty air.

They stick their rifles, here and there,
Right through him; meanwhile, he
Walks on toward Palmstrom, cheerfully.

IV

With the guard who brings in food
He enters the bare cell
Where his friend, the villain Palmstrom, has to dwell.

The guard, stuttering, stumbling, storms
Out, fabling of spirit-forms
Which he does not know how to master.

Men
Come running, in a body, then,
And hurl themselves on Korf—
In vain: Von Korf has ever been
Spirit. . . .

V

They find Palmstrom impossible to detain
(Though he himself has chosen to remain)
Since Korf's appearance cannot be turned off.

In some twelve jails, Palmstrom has been confined.
Everywhere, both directors and understrappers
Have very rapidly gone out of their mind.

At last, they conjure him with upraised hands
To choose for home; he'll have to go ahead
And not shoot anybody dead.

1913 55 die fliehenden Polizisten

The Fleeing Policemen

The Two Festivals

Korf and Palmstrom each hold a feast.

Palmstrom invites the whole world as his guest
But only on condition that they—fast!
Nothing to eat, all day, from first to last!
An antifaminefoundation is the rest.

Korf, though, goes through countryside and city
To the poor, to cripples, to the unfortunately vicious
And tries to make their spirits more propitious
Not being enraged, all day, by thwarted wishes;
Thus in their hearts arises a delicious
Every-foe-embracing pity.

Both, thus, permit Mankind not to receive
But give. Pleasures come, as they believe,
To creatures (who, after all, do
Think) only at such truly new
Festivities.

The Impossible Fact

Palmstrom, who is well preserved
Though getting somewhat feeble,
Is run down near a curve
By an automobile.

"How was," he asks and rises up
Determined to endure,
"Possible . . . such a mishap,
Yes . . . could at all occur?"

"Is the art of statecraft, relative
To motorcars, to blame?
Did police ordinances give
Drivers, here, free rein?

"Or was this trampling on the laws
To transform live men into dead,
Here? Short and sweetly, was
This teamster, here, prohibited?"

Swaddled in linens and damp gauze
He pores through ancient tomes of laws
And soon becomes clearly aware:
Vehicles Not Permitted There!

So he reaches this decision–
"This was a mere dream, for," he
Concludes with daggersharp precision,
"What *may* not, *can* not be!"

Fall

54

Gallows Brothers' Fraternity Anthem

Life on Earth, O gruesome tangle!
Here from our red thread we dangle!
The croaker croaks, the spider spins,
Snarled pates are parted by the winds.

O horriful terrors, fierce and foul!
"You are damned," so says the owl.
Against the moon's face, starlight shatters;
Are you so hard that nothing matters?

O horriful terrors, fierce and foul!
Hear how the silverstallions howl.
The screech owl wails: Yayhoo! Yayhoo!
Day too, will dew, will brew, will blue.

55

Gallowsbaby's Cradle Song

Sleep, baby, sleep,
In heaven stands a sheep;
The sheep is made of mist and dew
And fights life's battles, just like you.
Sleep, baby, sleep.

Sleep, baby, sleep,
The sun devours the sheep;
She licks it off the blue background
With her long tongue just like a hound.
Sleep, baby, sleep.

Sleep, baby, sleep,
Now it's gone, the sheep.
The moon comes out and scolds his bride
Who runs off with the sheep inside.
Sleep, baby, sleep.

Note: A parody of a very familiar German lullaby.

The Song of the Gallows Brother to Sophy, the Hangman's Moll

Sophy, my hangman's moll,
Come give me a kiss on the skull!
Though my jaw
Is a blackening maw—
Still you are a kind, noble girl!

Sophy, my hangman's moll,
Run your fingers over my skull!
Although the hair
's no longer there—
Still you are a kind, noble girl!

Sophy, my hangman's moll,
Come and gaze deep in my skull!
Though the eagle, no doubt,
Ate the eyes out—
Still you are a kind, noble girl!

57

Gallows Brother's Spring Song

Spring, even on *our* splinter, springs;
O sing for the blissful days!
Here, now, in the breeze there swings,
Now, over there, there sways

A young stem yearning toward the light
Out of a woodworm's bore.
I feel almost as if I might
Be what I am no more.

The Raven Ralph

The raven Ralph
        will will hoo hoo
he helped himself
        still still you you
with his own bill
on Gallows Hill
        will will still still
                hoo hoo

The Fog Gray Woman
        will will hoo hoo
coarse and common
        still still you you
she says eat up
it's good enough
        will will still still
                hoo hoo

But when at last
    will will hoo hoo
a year had past
    still still you you
there lay in red
the raven dead
    will will still still
        you you

59

No!

Rails the storm?
Wails the worm?
Howls
Where owls
To the towers swarm?

No!

It is the gallowsnoose
Loose
End rasps
As if, there,
Some outworn mare
Were driven to a gallop till
She must for the nearest water gasp
(Which might be distant, still).

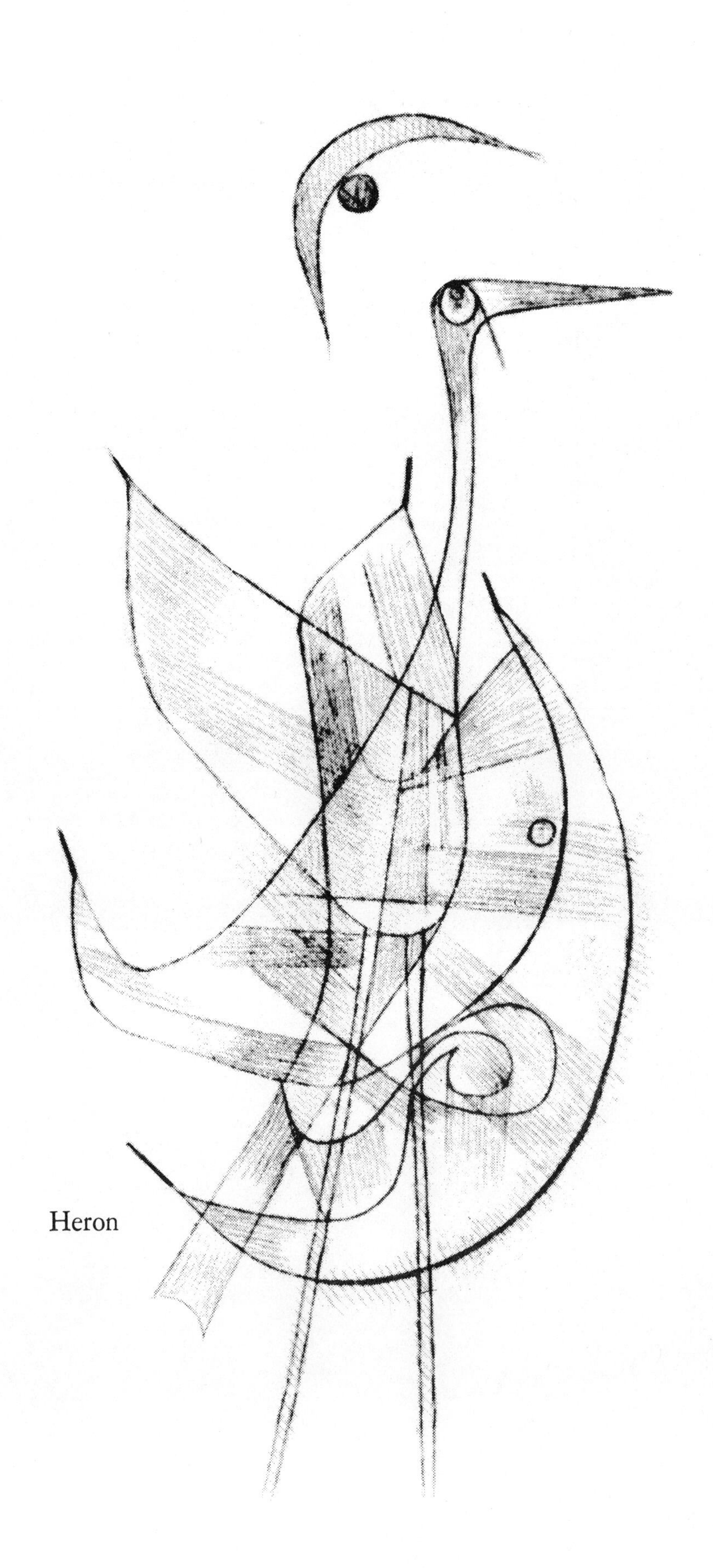

Heron

The Twelve-Elf

The Twelve-Elf raises his left hand:
Midnight tolls throughout the land.

The pond lies low, with opened jowls.
Softly, the Ravine-Hound howls.

Tensed in his reeds, the bittern stretches.
From his cold bog, the moss-frog watches.

The snail starts up inside his house;
And so does the potato-mouse.

Even the falsefires rest at ease
Lighting on wind-shattered trees.

Maid Sophie sees a vision, rare:
The Moonsheep at the Judgment Chair.

In wind, the gallows brothers sway.
In town, a child cries, far away.

Two moles, while midnight bells still boom,
Kiss on the mouth like bride and groom.

Meanwhile, dark on the lonesome heath,
An incubus clenches his teeth

Because a midnight-tramping shoe
Did not get lost in swamp or slough.

The Raven, Ralph, cries "Kraa! Kray!
Crack of Doomsday! Crack of Doomsday!"

The Twelve-Elf lowers his left hand:
Sleep falls again on all the land.

61

The Moonsheep

The Moonsheep stands in a vast clearing.
It waits and waits for the Great Shearing.
The Moonsheep.

The Moonsheep plucks itself three stalks
Then home to its high pasture walks.
The Moonsheep.

The Moonsheep dreams this declaration:
"I am the dark space of creation."
The Moonsheep.

The Moonsheep in the dawn lies dead.
Its corpse is white, the sun is red.
The Moonsheep.

The Sevenswine and the Rogue-o-Nights
or
A Happy Marriage

The Sevenswine and the Rogue-o-Nights
Received the matrimonial rites;
        Good people, shed a tear!
Their children numbered just thirteen:
First, the Hound-of-the-Ravine,
        While the next two were deer.

The fourth one was the Ravenmouse;
The fifth, a snail complete with house,
        O miracle divine!
Sixth, a screechowl, not too big;
Seventh was a Sevenpig
        And lived in Burgundy wine.

An armadillo, thick of hide,
Was eight; as soon as born, nine died;
        O sorrow and despair!
From ten to thirteen are in doubt;
Still, however, it came out,
        They're such a happy pair.

The Dance

An upbeat owl and a fourquarter swine
Meet where the shade of a column stands
In its creator's mind–
To the tune of Violinbow plants,
Grasping each other for the dance
By hand and foot, entwined.

On three pink legs
The fourquarter pig's
Skipping jigs exquisitely neat;
On her one, the owl's
Rocking her bowels,
Beguiled by the lyrical beat;
And the shadow still stays
And the fiddleplant plays
Tunes deliriously sweet.

Not iron, though, is the maker's brain–
And the column must fade as it rose.
Likewise our pair necessarily goes
Back to their nothing again.
The Violinbows
Now sweep to their close–
And no other clues remain.

The Shirt

You know the lone shirt, I presume?
    Fluttertata, fluttertata.

Its master has gone down to doom!
    Fluttertata, fluttertata.

It rattles and clatters when winds blow wild.
    Winduroodai, winduroodai.

It's weeping like a little child.
    Winduroodai, winduroodai.

        This is the lone
            Shirt.

65

The Lonely Rockingchair
on the Deserted Terrace

"I am a lonely rockingchair
And I rock in the wind, in the wind,
That moves so cool on the terrace where
I rock in the wind, in the wind.

And I rockle and knockle the livelong day
While knockles and crockles the linden.
Who knows what more might rock and sway
In the wind, in the wind, in the wind, in. . . ."

Heaven and Earth

Like a child, the nightwindwhippet cries;
Across his pelt the chilly nightsleet flies.

Wild, now, he's tracking down the Newmoonwife
Who, body doubled over, flees for life.

Below, one dot crosses a field, far distant:
There goes a Deputy Forester's Assistant!

67

The Old Wife with the Spindle

Through the silent rooms, barbaric
    Moonbeams gleam and kindle–
Lives in a narrow lane, far Arctic,
    The old wife with the spindle.

She moons and spins. What does she spin?
    Her wits out through the night.
She wears, to deck her body in,
    A camisole of white.

Through the silent rooms, barbaric
    Moonbeams pale and dwindle–
Lives in a narrow lane, far Arctic,
    The old wife with the spindle.

The Midnightmouse

It midnights; not a moon is out.
No star lives in the heavenhouse.
Runs twelve times through the heavenhouse
The Midnightmouse.

She pipes upon her little jaws.
The hellhorse from his nightmare roars . . .
Runs quietly, her allotted course,
The Midnightmouse.

Her Lord, the Spirit great and white,
Has gone abroad on such a night.
She keeps watch in his heaven; all's right.
The Midnightmouse.

69

The Moonsheep

II

The moonsheep tells himself goodbye,
I.e., he was thought over by
His own creator:
With one penstroke he yields all this
Up to his own self, as to his
Decapitator.

Fishes' Nightsong

—

◡ ◡

— — —

◡ ◡ ◡ ◡

— — —

◡ ◡ ◡ ◡

— — —

◡ ◡ ◡ ◡

— — —

◡ ◡ ◡ ◡

— — —

◡ ◡

—

71

The Nasobehm

Upon his noses walking,
Enter the Nasobehm,
Accompanied by his offspring,
You will not find his name

In Field Guides, the Britannica,
Not even in Audubon;
Out of my lyre, he first sprang
Into the light of Dawn.

Upon his noses striding,
As aforesung, he came
With all his young beside him,
The stately Nasobehm.

The Aesthetic Otter

An otter
sets his daughter
on gravel near swift water.

Do you know,
though, why?

The mooncalf, whispered low,
And told me, on the sly:

That sublime
-ly keen beast does
because
he can't resist the rhyme.

73

The Worm's Confession

Inside a shell
A worm does dwell
A worm of most rare sort
Who whisperingly,
Only to me,
Opened up his heart.

With all it uttered,
Oh, how it fluttered
And beat, his poor little heart!
You think I spoke
Just for a joke?—
Must you be so smart?

Inside a shell
A worm does dwell
A worm of most rare sort
Who whisperingly,
Only to me,
Opened his little heart.

The Hen

In the waiting room of the railway,
Not built for it,
A hen
Walks up and down.
Where, where has the stationmaster gone?
Surely no one
Will harm this hen?
Let us hope not! Then,
Out loud, let us say:
Our sympathy goes out to it
Even here,where it's in the way!

75

Die Fledermaus

(Spahouseconcertbeerterraceepisode)

The fledermaus
Heard "herself"—Strauss.

The moon appeared
Notably weird;

Her wings whisk past
The globed milkglass.

Ladies: "A bat!
Eeek, George! My hat!"

Whirr, whorr,—she flits
In someone's Schlitz.

At once a bus
-boy ousts her: - :thus - : . . . .

"Die Fledermaus"
Is done. No bows.

Porcupine and Porcupina

A porcupine sat on the lea,
On one quill piping tunefully.
Shalmeiala, shalmeialoo!
His truelove, Porcupina,
Came down to nyna-nina
To his sweet melody.
Spoonaleea, spoonalaya,
Spoonaleia, loo.

The beast's whole shirt was soon outblown . . .
She said, "How dreadfully strange you've grown!"
Shalmeiala, shalmeialu–.
Then ran off to the neighbor's. Eh!
He, by the brook, was washed away
To a distant pond, alone.
Lullalee, lullalei,
Lullalaya, loo.
Too too. . . .

77

The Horse

The bell rings for Professor Lee,
The cook is plucking chickens,
So Margaret goes: "Who could that be?"
        A horse stands on the doorstep.

So Margaret slams the door again.
The cook comes: "What's the matter?"
The lady, in her robe, comes then.
        The whole family comes along, too.

"I've come, excuse me," the horse ventures,
From Carpenter Johannson,
To bring, by way of my indentures,
        Your door and windowframes."

Fourteen folks and the pugdog stop
Like persons in a dream;
The smallest child, though, gives a hop.
        All the rest stand like treetrunks.

Since no one there will take his sense,
The horse just clicks his tongue;
And without one word more, turns hence,
Going back down the stairs once again.

All thirteen people turn to see
What thoughts their lord might utter:
"That was," declares Professor Lee,
"A remarkable experience."

Rosinante's Grandson

78

The Hack Horse

Although I only pull a hack,
I've kept up on philosophy;
Soon as the feedbag's round my neck,
I can't help ruminate, you see.
I swing it to, I swing it fro;
And with this mild, familiar swinging,
Through my brain such thoughts will go
As only wise men could be thinking.

Although I only pull a hack,
I've often reasoned, full of care,
How to get oats out of the sack
Into my mouth, from the depths, there.
I've swung it low, I've swung it high,
Until my very ears would ring;
What slept there, veiled in darkness, I
Found too deep for pondering.

Although I only pull a hack,
I need this consolation: I
Tell myself, thus foul and slack
Does all terrestrial knowledge lie;
In the Nosebag of the Profound
Every mouth partakes, perhaps,
And yet—Alas!—the Ultimate Ground
Particles evade our grasp.

79

The Vulture-Lamb

Lamb-vultures are known far and near;
The vulture-lamb is first named here.

Vultures are obviously heinous;
The lamb, however's, subterraneous;

Does not say "haa," does not say "boo";
Just gets close, then devours you

And rolls its eyes up to the Lord.
It is quite genuinely adored.

80

The Sandwich Paper

A sandwich paper, in the glen,
besnowed upon, feels cold and then

in its fear, although it never
before, in any sense, had ever

thought about thinking, naturally,
as a thing of rags, et cetera, be

-gan, from fear, as I just men
-tioned, thinking, started and commen

-ced to think—think what that means!—in fear, it
became, as I just mentioned, spirit;

that is, you understand, not mere
-ly down from up in Heaven somewhere;

rather, in consequence of a rather
precisely evolved gray brain matter

which out of wood, protein, flour, grease
(through fear) by skipping the otherwise

normal geologic ages, found
within this paper vessel and ground–

[within and on it found, by special
skipping of ages, ground and vessel].

Benefitted by this benefaction,
the paper decided itself toward action,–

toward Life, toward–started, anywhy,
to walking–like a butterfly. . . .

to creep, first, flying thereupon
till over the underbrush and on

up over the highway and criss
and cross and left, from that to this

the way such creatures turn toward Life
(as winds [or other things] connive)

And yet, dear friends! now blanch with me!—
a bird, quite fat and greedily

sees it (this is January. . . .)
and sets himself, both hide and hairy,

and sets himself both hair and hidey
(who could end here!) (Dear God Almighty!)

(consider how much was necessary!)
and sets himself, both hide and hairy,—

In the woods, a sandwich pape
-r, won, by fear, a natural shape. . . .

Enough! The wild woodpecker gobbles
The product, irrecoverable.

81

The Tortotoise

I am a thousand odd years old
And older every day;
The King of all Goths, Theobold,
Raised me on a tray.

The world's changed since, but all unknown
To my thought or my feeling.
Now for a small fee I am shown
By a businessman in Wheeling.

Death's voice, Death's face, I know not, nor
Conturbat timor mortis:
I am the tor- I am the tor-
I am the tor- to- tortoise.

The Unicorn

A unicorn will turn up sometimes still;
But only as a bar or grill.

At twilight time, each night, you stroll in there,
A regular, and take your chair.

Who knows? When many a year and day has passed
We may be like that beast, at last,

Merely hotels where they will go to eat (we
Will be spirits so completely).

Down at "The Golden Man" they'll sing and play,
Drink up, and pass their time away.

83

The Werwolf

A werwolf, one night, slipped away
From wife and child, and went directly
To the town schoolmaster's grave to pray
To that good man, "Oh please, inflect me!"

The town schoolmaster rose in air
Over his tin nameplate, and there
Spoke to the patient wolf who was
Sitting before him with crossed paws.

"Der Werwolf," said the good schoolmaster;
"Des Weswolfs, genitive, thereafter;
Dem Wemwolf, dative as it's called;
Den Wenwolf, accusative; that's all."

Flattered by the paradigm
The Werwolf rolled his eyes. "Meantime,"
He begged of the schoolmaster, "Do
Add to this my plural, too."

The schoolmaster had to admit,
However, he knew none of it.
Although great packs of wolves there be,
"Wer" exists only singularly.

The wolf rose tear-blind! How bewildering,
For he *had* a wife and children!
But since he was no scholar, he
Departed humbly, thankfully.

Note: "Wer" in German means "Who." We might get much the same effect by making this "The Hootowl." In that case, the third stanza would run:

"The Hootowl," said the good schoolmaster;
"Of Whosetowl's, genitive, thereafter;
To Whomtowl, which is in our native
Tongue, accusative *and* dative."

While lines 19 and 20 would go:

Although great flocks of owls there be,
"Who" exists only singularly.

which would gain an extra joke, but would lose the picture of the fierce, shaggy werwolf sitting before the village schoolmaster begging like a puppy and rolling his eyeballs with delight.

Gull Song

All the seagulls look the same:
As if Emma were their name.
They wear a great white paletot;
Buckshot will do to bring them low.

I never shoot a gull down dead;
I think about that with abhorrence.
I feed seagulls with good rye bread
And little reddish currants.

Mankind, no matter how you try
You'll never fly as seagulls fly.
If you're named Emma, be content
Resembling them to that extent.

85

The Two Donkeys

There was a donkey, feeling awful,
Told his helpmate, true and lawful,

"Oh, I'm so dumb and you're so dumb,
Let's just go die together—come!"

But as we note so frequently,
Both went on living cheerfully.

Klabauterwife's Letter

(Klabautermann: a spectral figure sometimes seen aboard ships shortly before they sink.)

Horribeloved Klabautermann,
My true beloved husband, thanks
For all the nice things that you wrote,
And that for four weeks more you will stay on.

The Marfa IS a lovely boat;
Just don't forget: The Devil's Banks.
My nerves are getting better here
Since, on the Elbe, nothing much goes on.

There is a Will o' Wisp lives near
With whom I now and then take tea,
But since she speaks Bohemian,
We can't converse, unfortunately.

6/1/04. City of Trautenau.
Your dutiful Klabauterfrau.

87

The Housemaid's Dream

The maid, this morning, talks—all wild—
"Last night I gave suck to a child;

Its head was a big cheese; and through
The hair, in back, a long horn grew;

This horn was made of salt, and what
Was strange, was good to eat; then. . . ."

"Shut,

Shut up!" the lady says "Now get
On with your business, Mar-gar-et!"

Margaret

II

Margaret has to clean the windowpanes,
Which is her grief, although the household gains.

"When one goes to my windows and looks out,"
The lady says, "he must be in real doubt
Whether the glass inside those windows is
Glass or mere air. Just you remember this!"

Margaret struggles with all of mankind's weapons
But simply can't create this air-resemblance.
Then gathering up her forces, with a shout
She finally smashes all of the panes to shivers!
Next, she picks, from the frames, the last few slivers;
This way is best, no shadow of a doubt.
At first, even the lady says, aghast,
"Well! Margaret's learning to clean house, at last!"

Yet very quickly one perceives what's so
And says unanimously: "That girl must go!"

89

Aunty Kunkel

Palma Kunkel is Palm's relative,
But beyond that is otherwise unknown;
And in the future, too, desires to live
Unknown, anonymous and quite alone.

Of Aunty Kunkel, as is only right,
This chronicler must also remain mute.
Only where she herself steps into light
He'll fully publish each step of her foot.

But she has not yet stepped out into light
And feels no least desire to in the future.
That her name's even mentioned here, is quite
Altogether contrary to her nature.

Ex Libris

An anonymous from Tibris
Sends Palma Kunkel an Ex Libris.

Upon it, nothing meets your sight
Except the white gleam of the light–

Not even one line to obtrude!
She feels she's warmly understood

And pastes these leaflets, pure and fair,
Gratefully in everywhere.

91

The Foresters' Station

I

Palma Kunkel, for her health, goes frequently on vacation
Far back in the woods to a lonely foresters' station.

From there, whenever a letter had to be carried,
Some laborer or a herdsman—whoever might have the
time to spare—he'd

Go to the game preserve that's near
And hang it upon the leg or around the neck of a deer,

Whereupon, in the following open season for that animal,
it would arrive, although with admitted occasional
tardiness,
First at the post office, and thence to its address.

The deer are proud of this honor; the neighbors, also;
No letter has ever been lost, far as we know.

The Foresters' Station

II

Long years ago were those words writ;
Today, however, that is no longer true.
Or insofar as it was first an owl, to who,
After deliberation, came this thought—to wit:
If one took care of the postal charge
Forthwith the shooting down becomes unnecessary.
Flying to the postoffice straightway from the sanctuary,
He was entered a "Carrier Owl" in the roster, white
and large.
Thereafter came the stag; next the hare;
At last, the whole game preserve stood void and bare,
For only business calls between the forestry station
And the postoffice were made by these former denizens.
Even if they pass through the old reservation
They are protected animals—"Postal Venison."

93

The Parrot

Palma Kunkel owns a bird
Who takes no thought to gain applause;
A parrot whom no earthly cause
Could make articulate one word.

The words he knows are numberless,
For he is quite the cleverest
Beast for sale from East to West,
Truly a gem of politesse.

No matter who you are, this bird
Inspects you with a steely eye
And yet his tongue seems to go dry—
He wouldn't give away one word.

"Polly"

"What's the parrot's name?" asks many a one,
But no one ever will tell anyone.

Somebody once addressed the bird as "Polly";
For weeks he fell in a deep melancholy.

He was restored and once again perked up
Only through a friend: Fritz Kunkel's pup.

95

Pollus

The still unbaptized poodle of Fritz Kunkel
Was purchased by Von Korf's step-foster-uncle.

He felt impelled when (generous to all), he
Heard of the sorrows of the so-called "Polly."

To her at once: and thereon, for her solace
He had himself, instanter, baptized "Pollus."

And, so to speak, took on himself the name—
By this deed putting all the world to shame!

Korf, himself, baptized him right away.
The bird was cured, moreover, from that day.

The Tomcat

Pollus, passing through this vale of strife,
Meets with the first tomcat of his life,

Who arches up his back, à la tradition,
Into a frightful circular position.

Pollus speaks with fearless tenderness:
"Pax vobiscum, gentle friend," he says.

97

Contrasts

Margaret is not beloved by "Polly"
Which leads to many serious incidents.
She, in the wench's presence, feels too fully
Their crass contrast in brains—and in good sense.

One hits the truth by saying, probably,
The life of this good maid, considered wholly,
Does not contain so much sagacity
As one calculus from the grey eyes of "Polly."

Pollus, however, is well disposed to her.
He secretly comforts the poor child; and at
Any time she's tired, will dust the furniture
(Using his tufted tail) in Palmstrom's flat.

Servants' Saturday

They hang them over the ledge,
The carpets large and small;
In mind they beat, they beat
Up masters, one and all.

With savage satisfaction,
Rage utterly berserk,
They cool their souls off for
One full week of work.

They batter Satanical rhythms;
Their rattans crack and split;
Front-of-the-house-type-ears
Take no account of it

But in back are wailing, torn
To the depths by whack and thump,
The runners, the Persian pillows,
And the featherbed, German, plump.

Bim, Bam, Bum

A belltone hurls through the night skies
As if with a bird's wings; he flies
In a Roman Catholic gown,
Far over meadow, hill and town.

He seeks the ladybelltone, BIM,
Who left him and has flown away;
A bad business; which is to say
She has betrayed, abandoned him.

O come, he calls, O come; your BAM
Is waiting for you here heartsore,
O come back, BIM, beloved lamb,
Your BAM adores you more and more.

Yet BIM, I ought to let you know,
Has given herself up to BUM;
He too belongs to Christendom,
Of course—that's just the trouble, though.

So BAM hurls on his headlong flight
O'er hills and forests through the night.
But all in vain—which is to say
Alas! he's flying the wrong way.

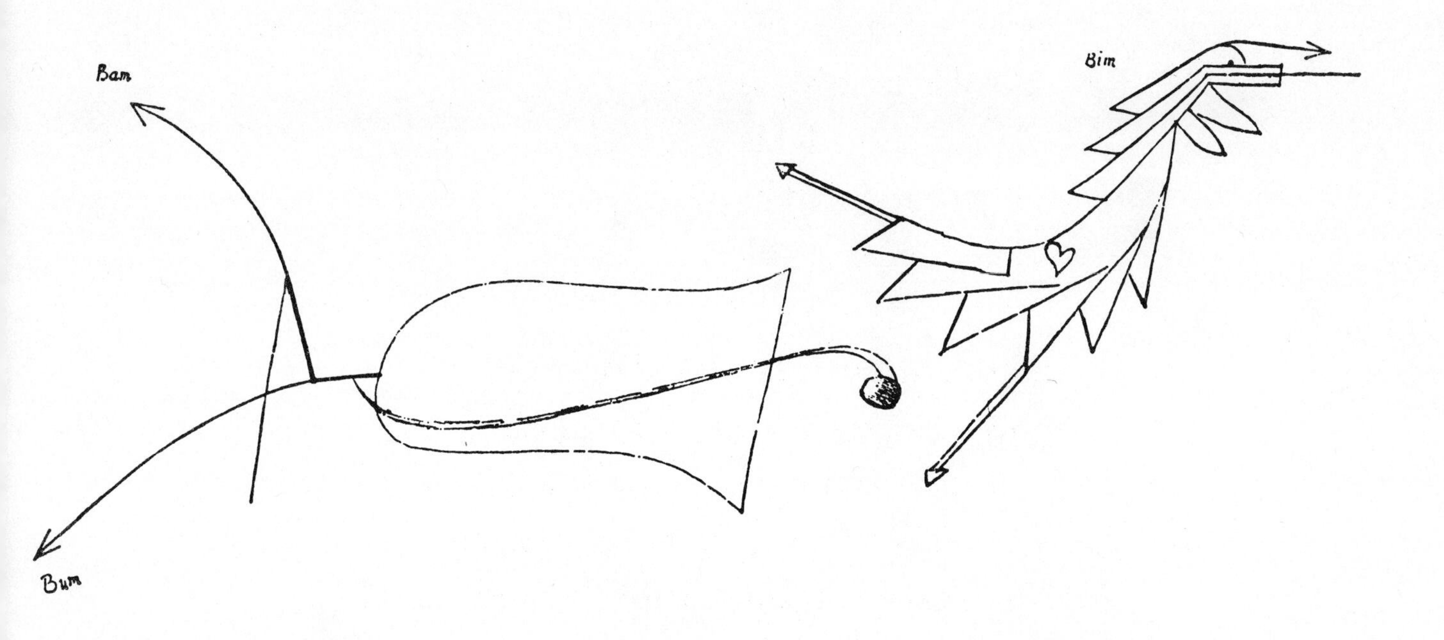

She-Belltone Bim

100

The Pike

Reformed by sainted Anthony,
A pike decided, morally,
Together with his wife and son,
To try and feed himself upon
The vegetarian ideal.

Since that day, he would only eat
Seagrass, searose and seaoatmeal.
Horrors! soon as he had dined,
Seagrass, searose, creamofseawheat
Flowed out again horribly behind.

The pond was soon polluted, wholly;
Five hundred fish expired in pain.
Saint Anthony, however, when
Hurriedly summoned back again,
Said only, "Holy, holy, holy."

101

The Experiment

For an experiment, I took
A darning needle from its book

And then obtained an old decrepit
Camel, who was still intrepid.

Nearby, I had a rich man stand
With two gold bags clutched in each hand.

The rich man, then, stepped to the fore
And knocked a knock on heaven's door.

St. Peter answered, "It is writ
A camel shall more easily fit

In a needle's eye than you could squeeze in
This enormous door, you heathen."

Firmly trusting the Lord's word,
I placed a sweet roll for reward

Just behind the needle's eye,
And shouted for the beast to try.

Lo! The animal passed through it,
Though squeezing himself like a newt.

The rich man, though, stared vacantly
And would say only, "Woe is me!"

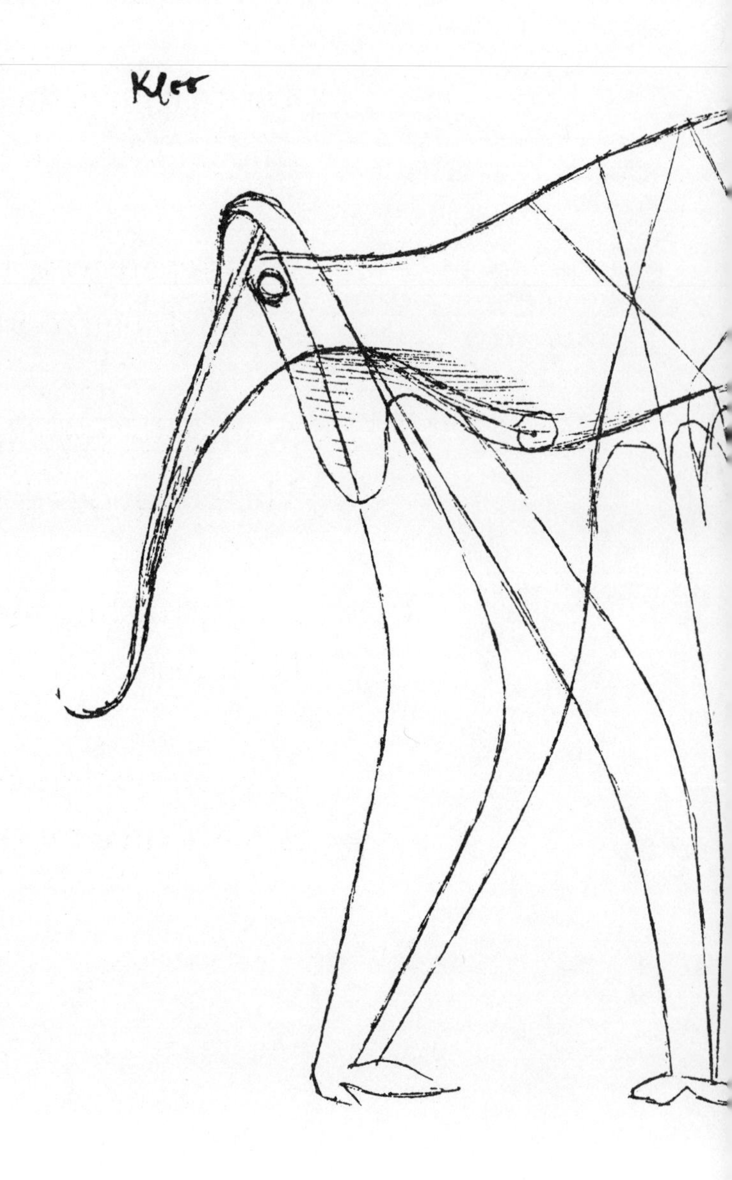

Midget He-Camel

The Painter

A painter, by his passions baffled,
Painted, in the apse's ground,
Satan, ferocious as a hound,
So Satan pushed him off the scaffold.

But lower down stood Mary, who
Out of the blue reached him her hand
And, so his foot had where to stand,
The pointed beak of her small shoe.

And spake to the young man: You see
How Lady Mary can repay
A rogue who flaunts himself today,
But painted her, once, beautifully.

103

The Rabbi

In Prague, a rabbi, name of Pelf,
Through Satan's magic came to gain
Such powers that even Death himself
Belched flames against him, but in vain.

In spite of all, though, Death won out:
He found a rose and hid inside.
Satan had not thought about
A rose; Pelf breathed her once, and died.

The Cock

Once a high magistrate in Basle
Threw a rooster into prison
For an act so reprehensible
It had the stink of Satan's kitchen.

Spurning the Lord and Nature's Laws
He'd laid an egg—as if to mock;
As if that weren't sufficient cause,
He seemed remorseless as a rock.

So he was haled to court and then
Questioned, tortured, doomed to the pyre;
Then fittingly, before all men,
They touched off, under him, a fire.

The cock cried, pitifully, "Kikriki."
Loud sang the encircling populace
Till someone called, "Fall to your knee!
Praise God! He cried 'Kyrieleis'!"

The Gramophone

The devil once approached the Lord
Carrying his gramophone
And said, no doubt a trifle snide,
"I bring the music of the spheres."

Listening to it squeak, the Lord
Seemed, for the moment, edified:
Truly, the universal tone,
In ghostly fashion, reached his ears.

But by the third time, this had grown
Revolting and absurd; the Lord,
Insulted, flung the gramophone
And Satan, too, infernoward.

St. Expeditus

Toward a convent full of nuns,
Some people, feeling kindly once,

Did as good Christians might and sent it
(Through Rome) packages large and splendid:

Apples and pears, cake and socks,
Some little bells, a music box,

Tools, aprons, shoes, warm underwear. . . .
Some boxes said: Handle with Care!

While some said only: This Side Up!
Some showed a black communion cup.

While there was painted, short and sweet, o
-ver each boxtop: Espedito!

Our nuns, who simply could not guess
Whom they ought to thank for this

Since the giver was unknown,
At first gave thanks to Him alone;

Still, though, they called out, without end,
On this well-intended friend

Until one morning Sister Pia
Suddenly cried out: "Santa Mia!

Not from Christian, not from Jew
Do such miracles ensue—

Dear siblings, no; his name must be
Expeditus; a saint is he!"

They all fell down then on their knee,
So the saint spake, saying, "See!

You've recognized me after all.
Now you must paint me on the wall!"

So they had a painter come,
A pious and Godfearing one,

Who painted there, with flawless art, an
Expeditus with the Carton.

His cult gained a wide following;
Whoever received gifts would bring

Small plaques for him, or candles tall.
Soon, he was in the hearts of all.

II

Suddenly, though in Ninteenhundre
-dfive, the whole world stands in wonder

Hearing the Church declare it can
No longer tolerate this man.

"Expeditus—" Rome insists,
"From this day onward, none exists!"

And since his dear nuns long ago
Have escaped this vale of woe,

He stands there and just looks about;
Not one soul in the world speaks out.

I only, at the Northern border,
Feel I am truly of his order.

Heretical, my pencil says:
Sanctus Expeditus—stays.

If his old portrait just won't do,
Here I'll paint his image new:—

Expeditus I then greet:
The Envoy I have yet to meet.

Expeditus, heavenblessed,
With hurrying feet that never rest,

With his locks of mild, white hair
And his manner debonair,

With his brown and kindly eyes
And big brown package to surprise

Children he visits while he strives
To mitigate their meager lives.

On top of this, I make so bold
To furnish him a halo, gold,

Which his smile scatters, on each hand,
Where he goes striding through the land.

Next, that their Angeljoy surround him,
I place his faithful nuns around him:

Maids from the groves of Italy
That shine forth pure and prettily;

The truth is, though, one of them goes
Far enough to thumb her nose:

Just into the "Bronze Gate," she's spanned
The littlest finger of her hand.

Yet, gushing from the Heavens above,
Swarm all the saints, the choir of love,

And blissfully sweet now sings Maria:
"Santo Espedito—sia!"

107

Golch and Flubis

Golch and Flubis, they are some
Conjurers from Titanium

Whom, once upon an evening, Zri,
The mighty Zra, bequeathed to me.

Suppose I lack for anything,
Should need a proof, a tree, a ring,

I send for Golch who has the knack
Of turning into what I lack,

While Flubis, his antithesis,
Becomes what you could gladly miss.

Should germs attack your tracheal tubis,
Your sore throat simply turns to Flubis.

Suppose that murder lays you low;
Death turns to Flubis, and will go.

How sweetly does one live with these
Golches and brave Flubises.

Let all men seek, assuredly,
The mighty Zra, aforesaid Zri.

The Knee

There wanders through the world, a knee
It's just a knee, no more.
It's not a tent; it's not a tree;
Only a knee, no more.

There was a man once in a war
Overkilled, killed fatally.
Alone, unhurt, remained the knee
Like a saint's relics, pure.

Since then it roams the whole world, lonely.
It is a knee, now, only.
It's not a tent; it's not a tree;
Only a knee, no more.

The Funnels

Two funnels go a-wandering through the night.
Through their narrowed trunks the white
Moonbeams flow to cast the better a
Light upon their
path
et
c.

The Sigh

A Sigh, over midnight ice, went skating,
Dreaming of true love and love's delight,
Beyond the tall walls of the town;
The townwall towers gleamed snow-white.

In his mind's eye, he saw a maiden
And stood still, glowing warmly. Then
The ice beneath him melted—down
He sank—and was not seen again.

III

The Picketfence

There was a picket fence between
Whose boards interstices were seen.

One night an evil architect
Turned up, just when you'd least suspect

And slipped out the interstices;
He built a spacious house from these.

The fence just stood there faint and quailing
With nothing on its naked palings,

A most disgraceful, obscene sight;
The Council banished it, outright.

The architect, though, got away
To Afri–or–Americay.

Opposite: Architecture in Ruins

The Underpants

Sacred are the underpants
In the wind and sunshine, freeing
Themselves from worldly circumstance,
Remembering their essential Being.

Joyfully rid of shame and hate
For this, their fundamental state,
They seem decorative details
Puffed faintly on their lines like sails.

Painter, bring all tropes in your power
To glory them and nothing spare—Ah!
They are your most faithful flower,
Fall, summer, winter, primavera.

Philanthropically

A nervous person with a meadow
Would be better off with none.
Let him discover how life can be led a-
    -way (in the main) from one.

No sooner will he have settled there
Than ants come, grasshoppers, worms,
Centipedes creep up; a bug's in his ear;
    Bees' buzzers sound alarms.

A nervous person with a meadow
Had better arise straightway
And go to another paradise instead o'
    Meadows (for instance, away).

114

The Twy

A most astounding creature, he.
He had his own head, and thereby
He had a second, at the knee
Which caused him to be called: The Twy.

In sleep or love, in drink or food,—
Routine concerns of livelihood—
The pair agreed most comfortably
By acting alphabetically.

More edifying, though, it brought
The holy processes of thought
Into the service of education
For all mankind's illumination

By giving itself clear and plain
Accounts of all its sensory data—
That is to say, of the same matter
Received in each respective brain.

Suppose this pair of brains, e.g.,
Reads a book (in duplicate), oh,
After each page, immediately,
Begins a dialogue just like Plato!

One day our hero strolls alone
With two bananas through the clover
Until he comes to a milestone
And sits, crossing the one leg over.

He eats, yet scarcely has he finished
When his spirit twice explains
Those sweetly silenced hunger pains,
Thus doubling his enjoyment's image.

Incredible; past all belief!
One body with a dual "I";
A person who nicknames himself,
Who looks himself straight in the eye.

115

The Two Parallels

There were two parallels went forth
Into infinity;
Souls straight as candles, souls of worth
And solid family.

To cut the other each was loathe,
Short of the blessed grave;
This was simply to them both
A secret pride and stave.

When, side by side, they both had wandered
Some fourteen light years more,
The lonely twosome felt no longer
Earthly as before.

Were they still parallels—they no
Longer knew aright—
They were like souls that only flow
Together through endless light.

Eternal light pervaded them
And so they came to be
One in it, like seraphim
Devoured by eternity.

The Stations

At stationstops for railways, near or far,
Mankind has the station-names called out.
In any place railroad officials are,
"Leetsdale," "Painted Post," or "Polk," they shout.
Such God-rewarded towns can well be proud
Living in tone, and not to stone confined,
For many times each day they ring out, loud,
United thus to the commuting mind.

Nights, only prowlers whisper otherwise,
Yet "Red Hook" and "Punxsatawney" are proclaimed.
You can see buttons, glimmering windows, eyes;
No hamlet is too tiny to get named.
"Barnesville" and "Zanesville" in the dark are known
Because of steam's great tendency to bind.
Towns off the side lie silent, though, alone. . . .
But that is God's will, too; just never mind.

117

The Stationmaster

The Station Master at a backwoods station
Feels great as any lord in all the nation.

A suburban, a mainliner, and a freight
At the same time (!)—that will be adequate.

In front, he tucks his hand into his breast
And looks about with true Field Marshall's zest.

He holds his arm, now this way, now that way:
Life has real significance today.

His heart would say to all that's greatest: Come!
Here is a man! Voilà! Un homme!

118

Memorial-Longing

Erect my monument, cherie,
All sugar, in the deep blue sea.

After my fall, I'll come to be
A sweetwater lake, just momently.

Yet time enough for several hundred
Fish to have drunk deep and wondered.

In Hamburg or in Bremen, then,
These fish shall pass the mouths of men.

And so I shall return to be
Part of your circles, properly.

But were I marble, brass or gilt,
Only some small bird would have spilt

His tailend, or I might be hit
By all some worthy person's wit.

119

The Lamp

A lamp, by the broad ocean, stands;
How, how has she come to these strange lands?

She wears a green seaweed sack dress
And stands on the Island of Askmeless.

The lamp, the lamp, the lamp—woe's me!—
Has come from the Whocannameit Sea.

On the ocean floor, a ship lies foundered;
Out of its ports stare salmon and flounder.

Waves, though, wafted *her* to these sands
Where, foot set deep, she dreaming stands

Wearing her green seaweed sack dress
While, in the background, lies. . . .Askmeless.

Ghost

There is a ghost
Who feeds on handkerchiefs,
Who will accompany you
Upon your voyage
And eat out of your suitcase,
Out of the bed,
Out of the bedsidestand;
Like a bird
Out of the hand,
Eat many things—
Not all things, not everything at once.
With eighteen handkerchiefs,
Proud sailor,
Did you set
Forth upon alien seas;
With eight to seven
Do you now return,
A sorrow to the housewife.

121

A Modern Fairytale

1. *Fruits of Education*

Cupboards open by themselves,
Spitting out from hooks and shelves
Dresses, trousers and tailcoats
With accessories of both.

Like some strangest dream they go
Through the chamber to and fro,
Drifting, striding here and there,
Quite as in their times of wear.

On the sofa or the chest
One will see them sit and rest;
At the table, by the stove,
On the chairs, in the alcove.

Here's a rare sight, and uncommon:
Headless, handless, men and women.
Yet one's properly astounded
That no softest word is sounded.

This tailcoat, and that little frock,
Keep still as any stone or stock;
Won't, as in the fairystory,
Call each other Frank or Lore.

No sound's made without a mouth—
They've been taught that from their youth,
So the waistcoat and the smock
Silently, with gestures talk.

The clock strikes one; the cupboards call
Come; may God forgive you all!
The wings bang to, with a loud clangor;—
Just one is missing from her hanger.

2. *Need Teaches Prayer*

Namely, that is, one blouse of lace
—Embarrassing case; O dread and shame!—
Did catch itself in that wild race,
Race of ghosts back to their house,
That is to say, one lacy blouse
Was hasped fast to the windowframe,
Salvationless and lost from grace.

In that dark house upon the frilly
Sufferer the moon shines chilly,
While she from the window tries to flee
Like one who dreams fierce demons chase
Her, yet can't take one step in space;
Within this room, the grim moon shrilly
Shines on this queer, crude scenery.

Then from another room nearby,
Lured there by her whimpering cry,
—For the blouse screamed, screamed piercingly!—
Now, from the next room does appear,
By her whimpering summoned here,
In from the next room swayingly
With slumber-fastened eyelids—SHE.

Who frees the poor creature, herself,
Unhooks it without more ado
And hangs it back up on its shelf,
Then slowly homeward sways off to
The next room, sways as creatures who
Are walking in their sleep will do,
Sways homeward to the room next door,
Home to her husband's side once more.

Shame

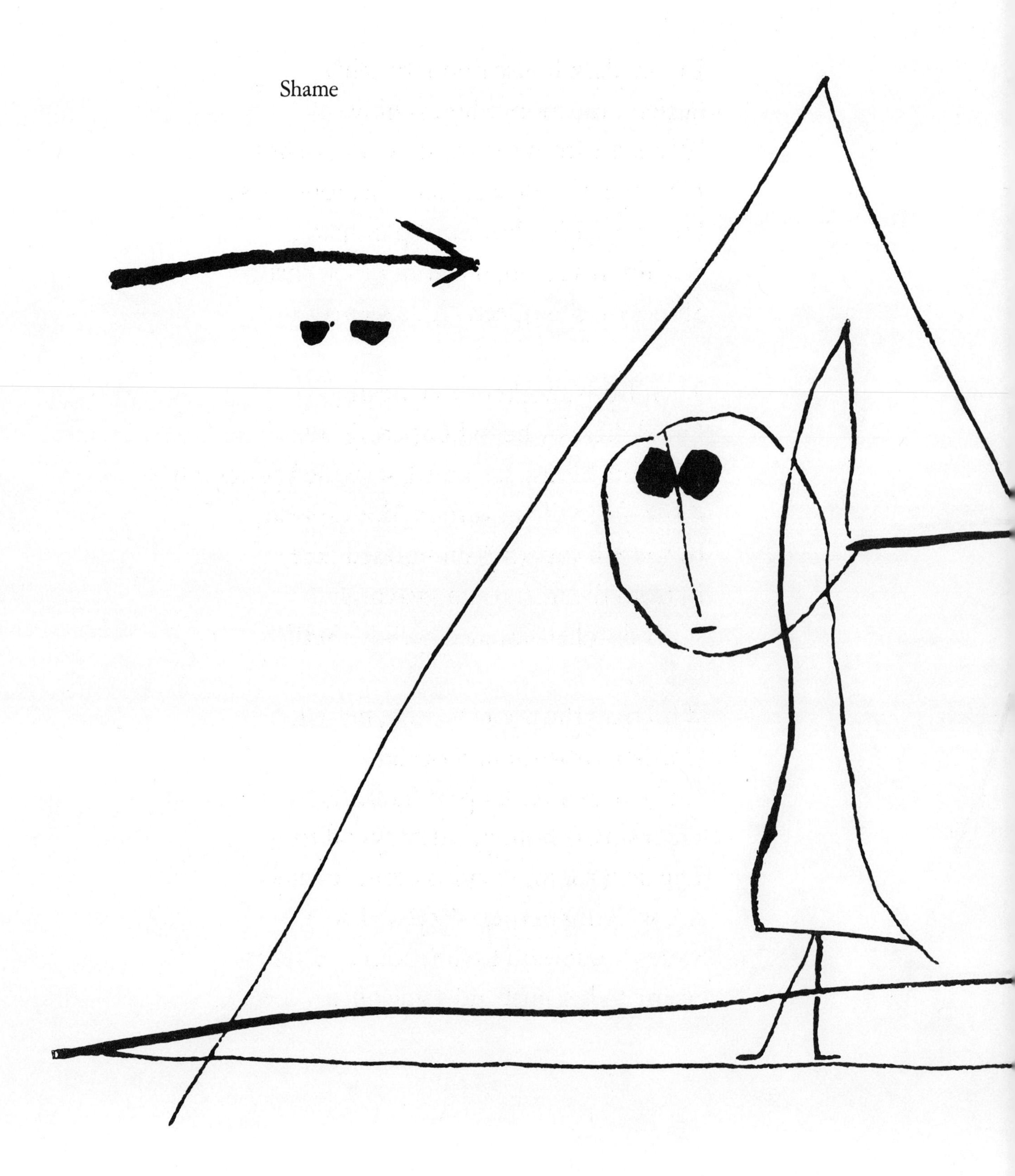

From the Suburbs
(To be Recited Soulfully)

I'm only a new street;
Not one house! Oh, disgrace!
I'm only a new street;
I look so out of place!

The moon peers from the clouds—
I say: But don't forget—
(The moon peers from the clouds)
I'll have some houses yet!

Already I own a name
Since yesterday—Fredericksthrone;
My sisterstreets, too, claim
To have names all their own.

The Messrs. Building and Loan
Have already let me in
Their confidence; honestly, soon
My building will begin.

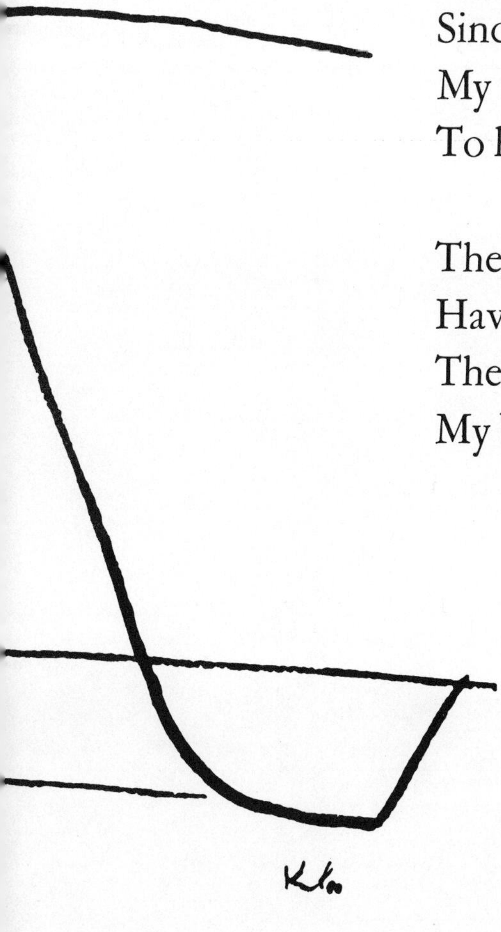

Shutting the door behind,
The moon goes as he came—
(Shutting the door behind)—
But look, I'm not to blame!

123

The Virus

A Virus crouched upon the terrace
Watching for someone he might harass,
Then hurled himself with malice fierce
Upon a human, name of Pierce;
While Albert Pierce could but respond, "Hey,
Shoo!" and had him till next Monday.

The Wallpaper Flower

I am a wallpaper flower fine,
Renewed, returning endlessly,
But not in May and bright moonshine;–
On all four walls. You'll never see

Enough of me. You will pursue
Me round your little room, unspacious,
Bounding as Knights of the Chessboard do,
Till you go nuts, my precious.